Contents

What's awake?

Some animals are awake when you go to sleep.

Animals that stay awake at night are **nocturnal**.

Foxes are awake at night.

What are foxes?

Foxes are **mammals**.

Mammals have **fur** on their bodies.

Mammals live with their babies.

Mammal babies drink milk from their mother's body.

What do foxes look like?

Foxes have orange-red **fur**.

They have black legs and white fur on their belly.

Foxes have a big bushy tail.

They have large pointed ears and a long **muzzle**.

Where do foxes live?

Some foxes live in woods.

Some live in hills or fields.

Foxes live where they can find food.

Sometimes they live near people.

What do foxes do at night?

Most foxes wake up just after dark.

They hunt for food.

Some foxes hunt all night.

Other foxes only hunt just after dark and before morning.

What do foxes eat?

In the wild, foxes usually eat rabbits, birds and mice.

They sometimes eat plant roots and berries.

In the city, foxes eat these things, too.

They also eat food from dustbins, bird tables or **compost heaps**.

What do foxes sound like?

Foxes can yelp and growl.

They may bark when they are angry.

Foxes call loudly to tell each other where they are.

They open their **muzzle** wide.

How are foxes special?

Foxes can hear very well with their big ears.

They can hear a tiny mouse squeak from far away.

Foxes can live in different places.

They can live near people or in the wild.

Where do foxes go during the day?

In the morning foxes find a safe place.

Then they lie down and go to sleep.

Sometimes foxes hunt during the day.

They do this if they cannot find food at night.

Fox map

muzzle

ears

fur

tail

Glossary

 **compost heap**
pile of old food

 **fur**
hair on an animal's body

 **hunt**
search for and catch other animals
to eat

 **mammal**
animal that has fur on its body and feeds
its babies with milk from its body

 **muzzle**
nose and mouth of an animal such as a
fox or dog

 **nocturnal**
awake at night

 **roots**
the part of a plant that grows
underground

Index